Origins

Micro Man Makes Big News

Emma Lynch
Character illustrations by Jonatronix

Contents

OXFORD
UNIVERSITY PRESS

In the news

Hello! I'm Tiger. I have a new school project.

We're looking at *journalistic writing* – that's the writing that you see in newspapers or in magazines. I have to choose a topic and find different types of journalistic writing about it.

At first, I didn't know what to look for. Then I remembered a very cool guy whose **exhibition** I went to this summer. His name is Willard Wigan and he's a **micro-sculptor**. He makes the tiniest sculptures in the world. He's been all over the news. I'm sure I can find some writing about him.

This is Willard Wigan holding one of his sculptures. It doesn't look much does it? You will need a **microscope** to see it properly!

What is a journalist?

A journalist is someone who gathers information on news and events. They write stories for newspapers or magazines, or they prepare reports to be broadcast on television, on the radio or on the Internet. Journalists are expected to present the facts about a story in a truthful and balanced way.

Journalists report on local events, national issues and things that happen in other parts of the world. Sometimes journalists will report on stories about people – about what is happening to them and about what they do.

Are you ready to take a look through a microscope at Willard Wigan's amazing micro-sculptures?

This is a sculpture of the Statue of Liberty seen through a microscope. It's small enough to fit in the eye of a needle.

Grabbing the headlines

Willard Wigan's work has been grabbing the headlines. Headlines are the words in big, bold type **LIKE THIS** at the top of a newspaper or magazine story. Headlines are usually in the **present tense**. They tell us what the story is about and should also make us want to read it. They need to be short and snappy to grab people's attention.

MICRO-ART MAKES SMALL FORTUNE

The world's tiniest sculptures today gained a massive price tag and pushed both collector and sculptor to the front of the art world. Former tennis player turned businessman, David Lloyd, has bought a 70-piece collection by the micro-sculptor Willard Wigan. The price paid by Lloyd is a secret, but the sculptures have been **insured** for £11.2 million, making the value of each one a staggering £160,000.

A delighted David Lloyd said, "Willard Wigan's work is an absolute inspiration."

What did they say?

Before writing a news story, a journalist will usually interview the people involved. This helps the journalist understand what happened and how the people felt. Newspaper reports often include direct quotes from the people involved in the story.

As well as giving their own views, people will sometimes tell a journalist what other people had to say. This is called *reported speech*.

QUEEN HONOURS MICRO-SCULPTOR

Willard Wigan with his MBE.

Micro-sculptor Willard Wigan today received an **MBE** for his services to art. Presenting the award, Prince Charles said, "Willard's work is phenomenal. I've never seen anything like it."

After the ceremony, Willard told friends that the MBE was unexpected and that he felt honoured and privileged to receive it.

ARTIST BREATHES EASY

Famous micro-sculptor, Willard Wigan, has finally finished his sculpture of *The Mad Hatter's Tea Party* after an unlikely accident wrecked an earlier attempt. Willard remembers, "One of the worst things was when I inhaled Alice. I was just putting her in position when I breathed in at the wrong moment and she was gone. That was nearly a month's work destroyed." *The Mad Hatter's Tea Party* is made from nylon fibre and is smaller than a speck of dust!

***The Mad Hatter's Tea Party* is now one of Willard's favourite pieces.**

Can you find examples of direct quotes and reported speech in these articles?

How does Willard Wigan make his micro-sculptures? How did he get started? I want to find out more! Let's see what I can find on the Internet.

http://www.willard-wigan.com

Willard Wigan: Friend of the ants

Willard Wigan is the latest hot talent in the world of micro-sculpture.

Willard Wigan struggled at school. No one knew that he had **dyslexia**. This made it very difficult for him to read and learn.

Some days, Willard didn't want to go to school at all. He hid in the garden shed. He watched a busy line of ants and decided to make them a home.

Willard cut tiny splinters of wood with a piece of glass. He built up the ant house using these bits of wood and some grass. Next he made the ants some little tables and chairs. He made them a playground with a slide and a merry-go-round.

The ants were not interested in their house. So Willard covered the floor and the slide with sugar and honey. He knew that ants like sweet things. Soon the ants were crawling all over their new home.

Willard decided there and then that he wanted to make more microscopic sculptures. For the next 40 years he would get better and better and his sculptures would get smaller and smaller ...

Using pictures

Another way to present a news story is using a comic strip. Comic strips tell us a story in pictures as well as in words.

This is the same story, presented as a comic strip. Which do you think works best?

Willard Wigan: Friend of the ants

Willard struggled at school.

He hid in the shed and watched ants.

He made the ants a tiny home.

He coated the home in honey.

The ants loved their new home.

Now Willard makes tiny things for a living.

Features

Journalists often write features about famous people and their work. Features look at a topic in detail. This feature **recounts** a visit to Willard Wigan's studio and describes how his sculptures are made.

At work with Willard Wigan

By Emma Lynch

Not many artists work in an area the size of a classroom table. But Willard Wigan is not like many artists. I have heard so much about his microscopic work that I have asked to see the place where the magic happens.

Willard's studio is in his Birmingham home, which is small, but not microscopic! Willard invites me in and shows me around. We toss a few nuts to Derek the squirrel, who spends a lot of time in Willard's garden and looks very well fed.

After we have had a quick play with Willard's remote-controlled helicopters (I counted more than 20 of them in the living room!), Willard leads the way to his studio.

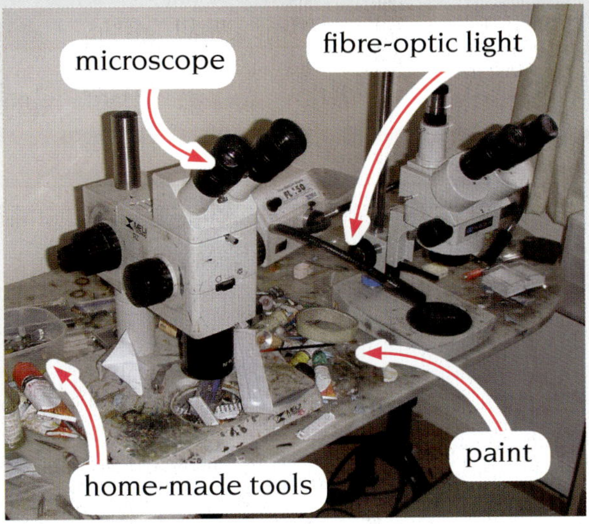

The small room is scattered with pictures and newspaper cuttings. Willard's desk is covered with the tools of his trade. His sculptures are made from materials as varied as:

- gold
- platinum
- dust particles
- sand
- human hair
- nylon
- zip tie (the plastic that attaches price tags to clothes).

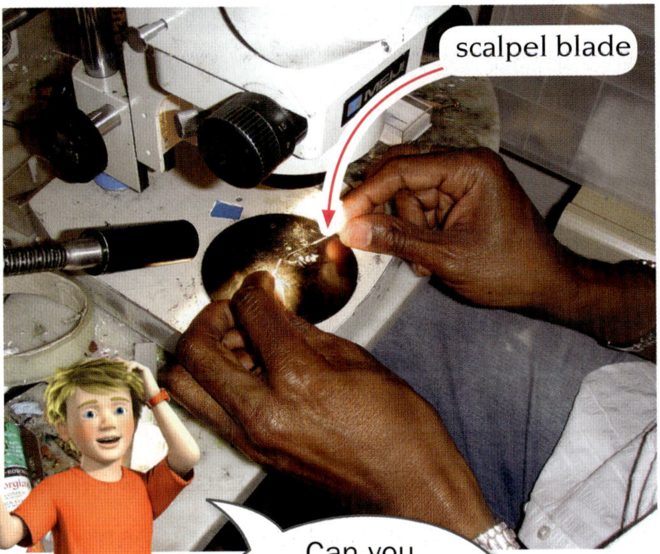

Willard has to work at night, when it's quiet, because the vibrations from traffic can disrupt his work and cause problems with the sculpting.

Willard makes his own tools. He grinds down scalpel blades and twists thin wires into hooks. He glues diamond **shards** to needles to make tiny blades. "Sometimes making the tools can be almost as hard as making the sculptures!" says Willard.

When Willard has finished sculpting, he uses thinned down oil paints to paint his pieces. He uses human eyelashes for paintbrushes, or pulls a hair off a dead fly's back! Willard's tiny sculptures can sit:

- on the head of a pin
- on the head of a match
- in the eye of a needle
- on a human eyelash.

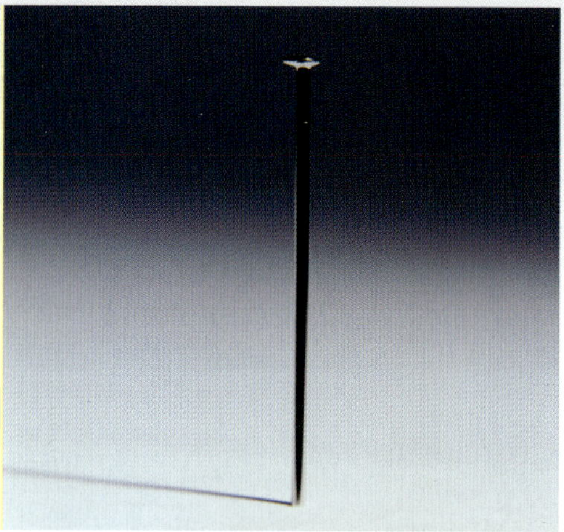

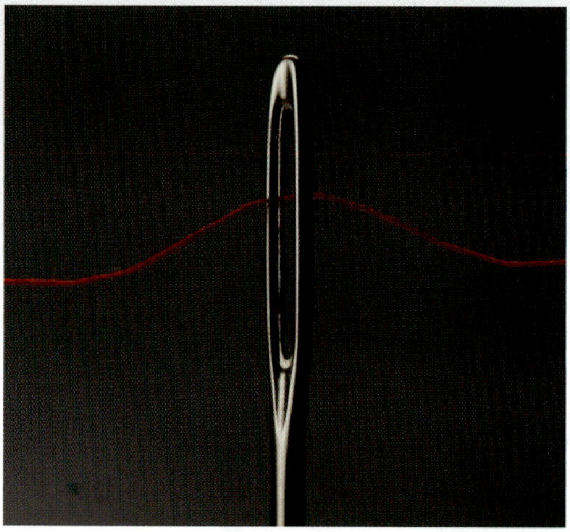

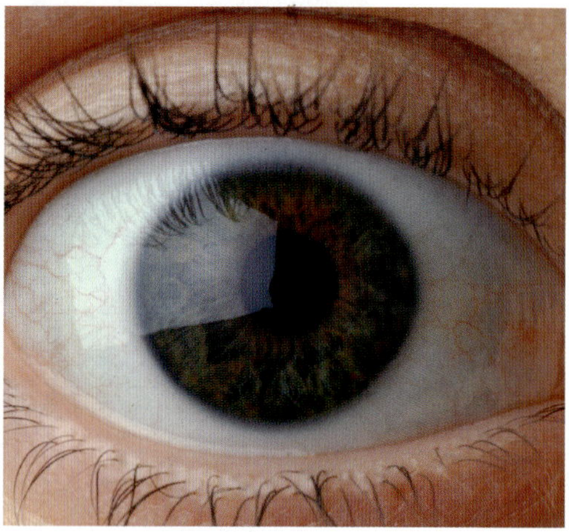

Willard's smallest sculptures can only be measured in thousandths of a centimetre. A human hair is about eight thousandths of a centimetre thick!

Willard brings out a couple of small boxes containing needles stuck in putty. He carefully removes a needle, slides it under the microscope and invites me to look. I am staggered by what I see. Little Bo Peep and one of her sheep stand in the eye of the needle, startlingly clear and beautifully brought to life. I ask to look at the needle more closely, without the help of the microscope. All I can see is an extremely small grey speck in its eye. It's incredible that anyone could have carved something so detailed on an area this size.

Willard invites me to try using the tools under the microscope. I find them very hard to hold, let alone use. My hands feel enormous! It is no wonder that **microsurgeons** ask Willard for advice and want to find out how he does it!

King Henry VIII and his six wives

Willard shows me *King Henry VIII and his six wives*. I am stunned by the detailed work on the faces and the clothes, right down to Henry's belt made of dust particles!

Question time

Journalists often interview people to find out information. They ask questions and the person being interviewed answers them. They might also take some photographs. The journalist then uses the information to write an article.

This is an interview with Willard Wigan – plus some great pictures of his work.

Q : Why did you start sculpting such tiny things?

A : It was **escapism**. When you've got learning difficulties, you find something else to do, to make up for what you can't express in writing. Back then, in 1962, teachers had a way of using you as an example. They took you round the school and showed the kids your work. They said, "If you don't listen to your teachers, your work will be like Willard's". They took away my confidence. It was like saying, "He's nothing and so is his work". I suppose I wanted to show people how big nothing can become.

Q : Can you tell me about one of your first pieces of micro-sculpture?

A : Yes, it was of a village. I had this twig and I could see a landscape in there, so I just carved it on there. I did that a long, long time ago now.

Willard carved Prince Charles and Lady Diana on matchsticks. Now his sculptures are even smaller.

Q : How do you do it?

A : I have to slow my whole **nervous system** down to do it. It's like **meditation**. I have to work between heartbeats. You can find the **pulse** in your finger if you search for it. That pulse can be like an earthquake and it can ruin a sculpture.

It's so painstaking, I have to have amazing self-discipline. I used to balance a ball bearing on my finger. I would train it to stay there for three hours and train my patience not to run out.

I can keep working now for 18 hours without stopping to eat or sleep.

You have to believe that what you're working on is the same size as yourself, that it's bigger than it is. It causes problems if you remember that it isn't.

This sculpture is of the English rugby player Jonny Wilkinson. He is standing on a pin head kicking a rugby ball through the eye of a needle!

Q : Do you enjoy your work?

A : I do my work for others to see. I don't get any pleasure in doing it because it's too hard! The satisfaction is when I finish. I like it when people see what I've done. People are stunned into silence. They say things like: "You must be an alien!", "How do you do it?", "It's not real, it's a trick!". I take it as a compliment when they don't believe that I did it – that's what makes me happy.

When you get a letter from the Queen saying how brilliant your work is, you know you're doing something right!

This is a photo of the Lloyd's building in London.

This is Willard's sculpture of the Lloyd's building on the head of a needle.

Q: Which is your favourite sculpture?

A: My favourite sculpture would have to be *The Mad Hatter's Tea Party*. I spent months on it then I lost Alice! When it was finished I was so relieved. *Charlie Chaplin* is another favourite. It's simple but it's powerful.

Q: Who are your heroes?

A: My mum's a great inspiration to me. She died in 1996, so she didn't see my full success. She knew it was coming, though. "The smaller your work, the bigger your name will be" – she told me that before she died. She used to say little things that meant a lot.

Another hero is **Martin Luther King**. I can relate to the problems he faced.

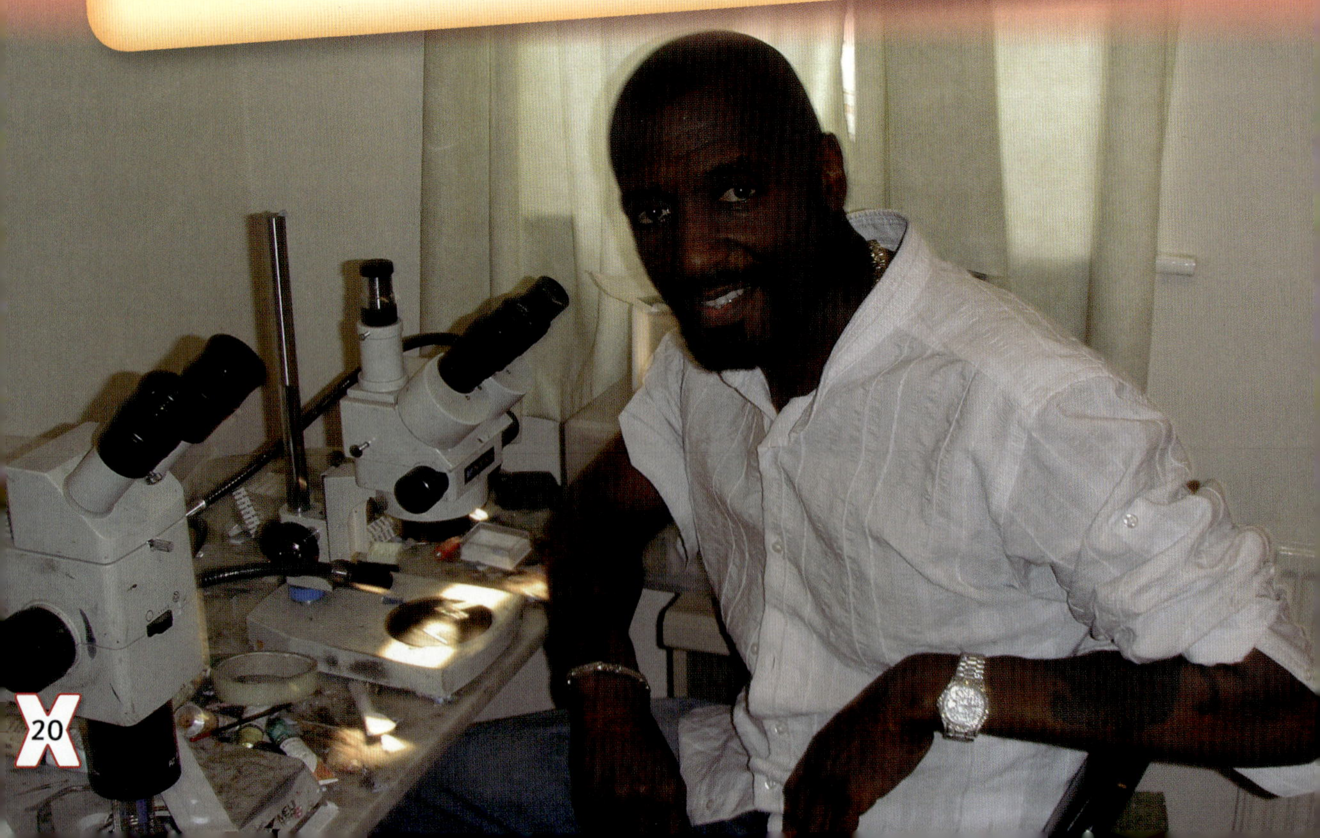

The Mad Hatter's tea party from the book *Alice's Adventures in Wonderland* by Lewis Carroll.

Willard's microsculpture of *The Mad Hatter's Tea Party.*

Q: Do you have any ambitions?

A: I have an ambition to do a masterpiece. I'm going to do the Queen's 1953 Coronation coach, with all the horses, on the head of a pin. I'm dreading it; I'm psyching myself up.

I want to go smaller. My work is too big. It's got to get smaller. I don't see it the way you do, it's still too big for me.

Q: What did you want to do when you were little?

A: I wanted to be the best artist in the world. I've become what I wanted to be. If you asked any successful person if they knew they were going to be successful, the answer would be yes. I knew from day one my work was going to have a colossal impact on people because it was so small.

This is a sculpture of a horse and rider on a pin head. Willard plans to sculpt the Coronation coach on a pinhead. That has eight horses!

Q: Do you like being famous?

A: I didn't set out to be famous. I set out to be successful in what I did. I wanted to make the teachers see what I'd become.

I look at life differently because of how I was treated at school. I don't **underestimate** anybody. I don't look at anyone and think of them as being less than me.

I still go on the bus. The driver is one of my fans! I just want to stay normal.

Q: How many of your sculptures would fit in a matchbox?

A: Millions! Probably six million ...

This is a sculpture of the characters from the film *The Wizard of Oz*. Do you recognize them?

This is a golfer practising his swing!
Would you like to be famous? What for?

Different points of view

Not everyone likes Willard Wigan's work. Not everyone believes it's real. It's a great topic for discussion and **debate**. What do you think?

London Bridge in the eye of a needle!

I don't think these pieces are art or sculpture. This is just some weird hobby. Art should be in picture frames, not under a microscope. Sculptures are made of wood or stone or metal, not grains of sand.

These are beautiful and creative works of art! Each of Willard's sculptures takes the most incredible patience, skill and determination to complete. They are so small but they still look life-like! If this isn't art, I don't know what is.

I just don't believe that Willard Wigan could have made these sculptures. It's got to be a machine doing it. How could one man make something so small? It must be a trick.. It's an obsession.

Of course there's no machine. This is definitely the real deal. Willard Wigan has given his whole life to creating these sculptures and to getting better and better and smaller and smaller. He's said himself that it's an obsession.

A final word from Willard himself:

My work is way ahead of its time. I'm not the only miniaturist in the world, but I've taken it to another level. I've taken it to an extreme that's impossibly hard to believe. I even ask myself how I've done it sometimes. But I did!

Some people think it's a hobby, some think it's art. I just want people to enjoy looking at what I do.

"I want to share my work with the world and I want to show people where I've come from."

Now I've got the hang of journalistic writing, I thought I'd write my own **review** of the Willard Wigan exhibition I went to. I hope you enjoy it.

Eye of the Tiger
by Tiger

Last month I went to see an exhibition of Willard Wigan's work at the Eyestorm Gallery in London. Willard Wigan makes very tiny sculptures, which is lucky because the gallery was pretty small! The sculptures are so tiny that you have to look at them through a very strong microscope.

When you look through the microscope it's totally mind-blowing. Suddenly you see an amazingly clear little sculpture below you. The colours are so bright and the characters are really life-like. I saw microscopic versions of The Statue of Liberty and King Henry VIII. My favourite sculpture had to be the tiger!

The sculptures take loads of skill to make and Willard Wigan has spent his life practising. Willard's lifetime collection has been bought by a man called David Lloyd, who is going to show his work around the world. Willard is going on to bigger, or should that be smaller, things!

My favourite Willard Wigan sculpture.

Find out more

Well, that's my project sorted. It's amazing what you can do when you're really interested in something! I hope you've enjoyed finding out about Willard Wigan as much as I have.

You can find out more about Willard and the work of other micro-sculptors on the Internet.

Find out more about Willard Wigan and his micro-sculptures, at www.willard-wigan.com

Can you name these two famous characters?

Search the Internet to find out more about micro-sculpture and miniaturists. Uncover the work of Hagop Sandaljian and Edward Kazarian. You'll be amazed when you see Sandaljian's version of *Snow White and the Seven Dwarves* sitting on a needle!

See if you can discover the miniature world of Nikolai Syadristy. His incredible micro-sculptures include a full chess set on a pin head!

Glossary

debate	a formal discussion normally involving several people
dyslexia	when someone has difficulty reading letters or words
escapism	getting away from things by doing something else
exhibition	a group of things put on show so that people can come and see them
insure	to pay money to a company so that if something was lost, stolen or damaged, they will give you money back for it
Martin Luther King	a leader of the American civil rights movement who fought for equal rights for black people
MBE	an award given out by the Queen
meditation	to think carefully about something or to relax your mind
microscope	an instrument that makes it possible for you to see really tiny things by making them look much bigger
micro-sculptor	someone who makes very small works of art
microsurgeon	someone who performs surgery using magnifying equipment
nervous system	the system of nerves in your body which carries messages to and from your brain
present tense	to write as if it is happening now
pulse	the throbbing you can feel in a vein as blood is pumped round your body
recount	to tell or to retell something
review	a written report
shard	a sharp piece of broken glass, metal or pottery
underestimate	to give something less importance than it really has

Index